Everything About

Handwriting

Everything you need for learning success!

Carson-Dellosa Publishing LLC
Greensboro, North Carolina

Carson-Dellosa Publishing LLC
P.O. Box 35665
Greensboro, NC 27425 USA

ISBN 978-1-62399-100-5

01-002137811

Table of Contents

Practice by tracing the lines.

Name _Danice_

Practice by tracing the lines.

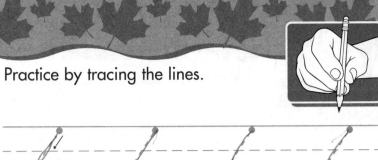

Name _____

Practice by tracing the lines.

Name _____

Practice by tracing the lines.

Name _____

Practice by tracing the lines.

Name _____

Practice by tracing the lines.

Name _____

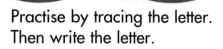

Aa

Practise by tracing the letter.
Then write the letter.

Name _____

A A A A A A A A

a a a a a a a

Practise by tracing the words.
Then write the words.

Name _____

alligator

apple

ant

Allison

Write the phrase.

Name _____

Alligators and ants

eat apples   *eat apples*

Write the sentence.

Name _____

Alligators and ants

eat apples.

Bb

Practise by tracing the letter.
Then write the letter.

Name _____

B B B B B B B

b b b b b b b

Practise by tracing the words.
Then write the words.

Name _____

bear

ball

bee

Bobby

Bb

Name _____

Brave Bobby

baseball bat

Write the sentence.

Name _____

Brave Bobby buys a baseball bat.

Cc

Practise by tracing the letter.
Then write the letter.

Name _____

C C C C C C C

c c c c c c c

Practise by tracing the words.
Then write the words.

Name _____

cats

cookies

cards

Chuck

Write the phrase.

Name _____

cool cats

play cards

Write the sentence.  Name _____

Cool cats play cards.

Dd

Practise by tracing the letter.
Then write the letter.

Name _____

D D D D D D D

d d d d d d d

Practise by tracing the words.
Then write the words.

Name _____

duck

dog

dance

Danny

Dd

Name _____

Danny dances

dandy dog

Write the sentence.

Name _____

Danny dances with a dandy dog.

Ee

Practise by tracing the letter.
Then write the letter.

Ee

Practise by tracing the words.
Then write the words.

Name _____

elephant

egg

elbow

Ellie

Ee

Write the phrase.

Name _____

Every evening

Ellie eats

Write the sentence.

Name _____

Every evening Ellie eats

eggs.

Ff

Practise by tracing the letter.
Then write the letter.

Name _____

Ff

Practise by tracing the words.
Then write the words.

Name _____

frog

fish

fox

Frank

Ff

Name _____

Four foxes

Five fish

Write the sentence.

Name _____

Four foxes and five fish fly to Frank's farm.

Gg

Practise by tracing the letter.
Then write the letter.

Name _____

G G G G G G G

g g g g g g g

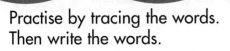

Practise by tracing the words.
Then write the words.

Name _____

giraffe

grass

glasses

Gretchen

Gg

Write the phrase.

Name _____

Gretchen wears

grey glasses

Write the sentence.

Name _____

Gretchen wears grey glasses.

Practise by tracing the letter.
Then write the letter.

Name _____

Practise by tracing the words.
Then write the words.

Name _____

hippo

hat

heart

Hannah

Hh

Hannah hears

hungry hippo

Write the sentence.  Name _____

Hannah hears a hungry hippo.

Practise by tracing the letter.
Then write the letter.

Name _____

Practise by tracing the words.
Then write the words.

Name _____

ink

iguana

igloo

Iceland

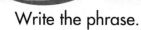

Write the phrase.

Name _____

Iguanas itch

in Iceland

Write the sentence.

Name _____

Iguanas itch in Iceland.

Jj

Practise by tracing the letter.
Then write the letter.

Name _____

Practise by tracing the words.
Then write the words.

Name _____

jaguar

jump

jam

June

Jj

Write the phrase.

Name _____

Jumping jaguars

jolly jokes

Write the sentence.  Name _____

Jumping jaguars tell jolly jokes.

Kk

Practise by tracing the letter.
Then write the letter.

Name _____

Practise by tracing the words.
Then write the words.

Name _____

kangaroo

kite

key

Kelsey

Kk

Kind Kelsey

keeps kangaroos

Write the sentence.  Name _____

Kind Kelsey keeps kangaroos.

Practise by tracing the letter.
Then write the letter.

Name _____

Practise by tracing the words.
Then write the words.

Name _____

lion

lollipop

lick

Lori

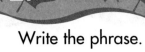
Write the phrase.

Name _____

Little Lori

likes lions

Write the sentence.

Name _____

Little Lori likes lions and lollipops.

Mm

Practise by tracing the letter.
Then write the letter.

Name _____

M M M M M M M M

m m m m m m m m

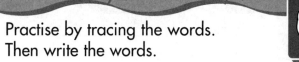

Practise by tracing the words.
Then write the words.

Name _____

monkey

mushroom

moon

Megan

Mm

Write the phrase.

Name _____

Mommy monkeys

Megan's mushrooms

Write the sentence.  Name _____

Mommy monkeys mash
Megan's mushrooms.

Nn

Practise by tracing the letter.
Then write the letter.

Name _____

N N N N N N N N

n n n n n n n

Practise by tracing the words.
Then write the words.

Name _____

newt

nest

note

Norfolk

Nn

Name _____

Nine newts

no nest

Write the sentence.  Name _____

Nine newts have no nest.

Oo

Practise by tracing the letter.
Then write the letter.

Name _____

Practise by tracing the words.
Then write the words.

Name _____

ostrich

octopus

olive

Olivia

Oo

Write the phrase.

Name _____

Olivia owns

one ostrich

Write the sentence.

Name _____

Olivia owns one ostrich and one octopus.

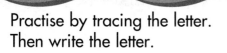

Pp

Practise by tracing the letter.
Then write the letter.

P P P P P P P

p p p p p p p

Practise by tracing the words.
Then write the words.

Name _____

penguin

pizza

pencil

puppy

Pp

puppy plays

pretty pool

Write the sentence.

Name _____

The puppy plays in the pretty pool.

Qq

Practise by tracing the letter.
Then write the letter.

Name _____

Q Q Q Q Q Q Q

q q q q q q q

Practise by tracing the words.
Then write the words.

Name _____

quail

queen

quarter

quit

Qq

Write the phrase.

Name _____

quiet queen

quits quarreling

Write the sentence.  Name _____

The quiet queen quits quarreling.

Rr

Practise by tracing the letter.
Then write the letter.

Name _____

R R R R R R R R

r r r r r r r r

Practise by tracing the words.
Then write the words.

Name _____

rabbit

ribbon

race

runs

Rr

Write the phrase.

Name _____

rabbits run

road race

Write the sentence.  Name _____

Rowdy rabbits run a road
race.

Ss

Practise by tracing the letter.
Then write the letter.

Name _____

S S S S S S S

S S S S S S S

Practise by tracing the words.
Then write the words.

Name _____

seal

sun

shell

seven

Ss

Write the phrase.

Name _____

Seven shells

soft sunshine

Write the sentence.  Name _____

Seven shells shine in the soft sunshine.

Tt

Practise by tracing the letter.
Then write the letter.

Name _____

Practise by tracing the words.
Then write the words.

Name _____

turtle

tiger

tie

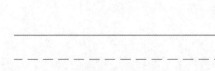

teach

Tt

Name _____

Ten turtles

teach tigers

Write the sentence.

Name _____

Ten turtles teach tigers.

Uu

Practise by tracing the letter.
Then write the letter.

Name _____

U U U U U U U

u u u u u u u

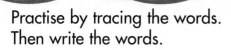
Practise by tracing the words.
Then write the words.

Name _____

umpire

umbrella

under

unhappy

Uu

Unhappy umpires

ugly umbrellas

Write the sentence.

Name _____

Unhappy umpires use ugly umbrellas.

Vv

Practise by tracing the letter.
Then write the letter.

Name _____

Practise by tracing the words.
Then write the words.

Name _____

vulture

violin

vest

van

Vv

Name _____

Vultures in vests

play violins

Write the sentence.

Name _____

Vultures in vests play violins.

Ww

Practise by tracing the letter.
Then write the letter.

Name _____

Practise by tracing the words.
Then write the words.

Name _____

whale

walrus

water

wishes

Ww

Write the phrase.

Name _____

walrus wishes

warm water

Write the sentence.

Name _____

A walrus wishes for warm water.

Xx

Name _____

X X X X X X X

X X X X X X X

Practise by tracing the words.
Then write the words.

Name _____

X-ray

Xylophone

Max

Extra

Xx

Name _____

extra saxophone

extra xylophone

Write the sentence.  Name _____

Max got extra xylophones
and saxophones.

Yy

Practise by tracing the letter.
Then write the letter.

Name _____

Practise by tracing the words.
Then write the words.

Name _____

yak

yo-yo

yarn

Your

Yy

Name _____

Your yak

Yellow yo-yo

Write the sentence.

Name _____

Your yak plays with a yellow yo-yo.

Zz

Practise by tracing the letter.
Then write the letter.

Name _____

Practise by tracing the words.
Then write the words.

Name _____

zebra

zipper

zoo

zigzag

Zz

Name _____

zany zebras

zigzag zoo

Write the sentence.  Name _____

Zany zebras zigzag through the zoo.

Practise by tracing the words and
numbers. Then write the words
and numbers.

Name _____

one 1

two 2

three 3

four 4

five 5

Practise by tracing the words and numbers. Then write the words and numbers.

Name _____

six 6

seven 7

eight 8

nine 9

ten 10

Practise by tracing the words and
numbers. Then write the words
and numbers.

Name _____

eleven 11

twelve 12

thirteen 13

fourteen 14

fifteen 15

Practise by tracing the words and numbers. Then write the words and numbers.

Name _____

sixteen 16

seventeen 17

eighteen 18

nineteen 19

twenty 20

Complete these sentences:

Name _____

I have _____ people in my family.

I have _____ students in my classroom.

I go to school at ___ o'clock.

For an after-school snack, I eat _____ grapes.

Practise by tracing the words.
Then write the words.

Name _____

square

circle

rectangle

oval

Practise by tracing the words.
Then write the words.

Name _____

red

blue

yellow

orange

Practise by tracing the words.
Then write the words.

Name _____

black

white

purple

pink

Colour Words

Practise by tracing the words.
Then write the words.

Name _____

brown

grey

green

Complete this sentence:

My favourite colour

is _____.

Name _____

Practise by tracing the words and abbreviations. Then write the words and abbreviations.

Sunday

Sun.

Monday

Mon.

Days of the Week
and Abbreviations

Practise by tracing the words and abbreviations. Then write the words and abbreviations.

Name _____

Tuesday

Tues.

Wednesday

Wed.

Practise by tracing the words and abbreviations. Then write the words and abbreviations.

Name _____

Thursday

Thurs.

Friday

Fri.

Days of the Week
and Abbreviations

Practise by tracing the words and abbreviations. Then write the words and abbreviations.

Name _____

Saturday

Sat.

Today

Complete these sentences:

Name _____

Today is _____.

My birthday is _____.

The 100th day of school

is _____.

Canada Day is

celebrated on _____.

Months of the Year
and Abbreviations

Practise by tracing the words and abbreviations. Then write the words and abbreviations.

Name _____

January

Jan.

February

Feb.

Practise by tracing the words and abbreviations. Then write the words and abbreviations.

Name _____

March

Mar.

April

Apr.

Months of the Year
and Abbreviations

Practise by tracing the words and abbreviations. Then write the words and abbreviations.

Name _____

May

June

July

August

Aug.

Practise by tracing the words and abbreviations. Then write the words and abbreviations.

Name _____

September

Sept.

October

Oct.

Practise by tracing the words and
abbreviations. Then write the words
and abbreviations.

Name _____

November

Nov.

December

Dec.

Practise by tracing the words.
Then write the words.

Name _____

winter

spring

summer

fall

Weather Words

Practise by tracing the words.
Then write the words.

Name _____

snow

rain

sunshine

sleet

Complete this sentence:

Outside I see _____.

Complete these sentences:

Name _____

Snow falls in_____.

Flowers bloom in_____.

In the _____,

we go swimming.

In the _____, leaves fall.

Practise by tracing the words.
Then write the words.

Name _____

Halloween

Easter

Canada Day

Hanukkah

Practise by tracing the words.
Then write the words.

Name _____

Christmas

Valentine's Day

Kwanza

Happy Birthday

Practise by tracing the words.
Then write the words.

Name _____

gym

playground

classroom

principal's office

Practise by tracing the words.
Then write the words.

Name _____

math

music

art

gym

Practise by tracing the words.
Then write the words.

Name _____

science

spelling

social studies

writing

Practise by tracing the words.
Then write the words.

Name _____

teacher

aide

nurse

principal

Complete these sentences:

Name _____

My teacher's name is

_____.

My school is called

_____.

My classroom is _____.

Complete these sentences:

Name _____

My principal's name is

_____.

My favourite subject is

_____.

I am in grade _____.

Practise by tracing the words.
Then write the words.

Name _____

pencil

book

folder

paper

Practise by tracing the words.
Then write the words.

Name _____

awesome

excellent

way to go

great

Practise by tracing the words.
Then write the words.

Name _____

stop

go

caution

Complete these sentences:

Name _____

A _____ light means go.

A _____ light means stop.

A _____ light means

caution.

Practise by tracing the words.
Then write the words.

Name _____

Mother

Father

Mom

Practise by tracing the words.
Then write the words.

Name _____

Dad

Grandma

Grandpa

Practise by tracing the words.
Then write the words.

Name _____

aunt

uncle

brother

sister

Write the names of the people
in your family.

Name _____

Practise by tracing the words.
Then write the words.

Name _____

street

road

store

theatre

Practise by tracing the words.
Then write the words.

Name _____

apartment

library

office

park

Complete these sentences:

Name _____

I live in a _____.

My address is _____

_____

Write a sentence about your neighbourhood:

_____

_____

_____

_____

_____

_____

_____

Practise by tracing the words.
Then write the words.

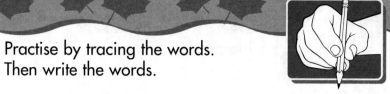

Name _____

country

city

province

territory

Complete these sentences:

Name _____

My country is _____

_____ .

My province or territory is

_____ .

My city is _____

_____ .

Practise by tracing the words.
Then write the words.

Name _____

bread

meat

vegetable

fruit

Practise by tracing the words.
Then write the words.

Name _____

soup

sandwich

cake

ice cream

Complete these sentences:

Name _____

My favourite foods are:

If I had a restaurant, this would be my menu:

Direction Words

Practise by tracing the words.
Then write the words.

Name _____

right

left

up

down

Practise by tracing the words.
Then write the words.

Name _____

over

under

beside

behind

Practise by tracing the words.
Then write the words.

Name _____

soccer

football

baseball

golf

Practise by tracing the words.
Then write the words.

Name _____

basketball

swimming

volleyball

karate

Practise by tracing the words.
Then write the words.

Name _____

goal

point

team

run

Practise by tracing the words.
Then write the words.

Name _____

coach

score

guard

Complete this sentence:

My favourite sport is

_____.

Practise by tracing the words.
Then write the words.

Name _____

dollar $

cents ¢

penny 1¢

Practise by tracing the words.
Then write the words.

Name _____

nickel 5¢

dime 10¢

quarter 25¢

Write the correct word under the correct coin.

Name _____

_____

- - - - - - - - - - - - - - -

_____

_____

- - - - - - - - - - - - - - -

_____

_____

- - - - - - - - - - - - - - -

_____

_____

- - - - - - - - - - - - - - -

_____

_____

- - - - - - - - - - - - - - -

_____

_____

- - - - - - - - - - - - - - -

_____

_____

- - - - - - - - - - - - - - -

_____

_____

- - - - - - - - - - - - - - -

_____

_____

- - - - - - - - - - - - - - -

_____

_____

- - - - - - - - - - - - - - -

_____

Practise by tracing the words.
Then write the words.

Name _____

run

swim

jump

fly

Practise by tracing the words.
Then write the words.

Name _____

sing

read

play

study

Practise by tracing the words.
Then write the words.

Name _____

big

long

tall

good

Comparison Adjectives

Write the correct adjective next to the picture.

Name _____

tall

taller

tallest

Write the correct adjective next to the picture.

Name _____

big

bigger

biggest

Write the correct adjective
next to the picture.

Name _____

small

smaller

smallest

_____
- - - - - - - - - - - - - - - - - - -
_____

_____
- - - - - - - - - - - - - - - - - - -
_____

_____
- - - - - - - - - - - - - - - - - - -
_____

Write the correct adjective
next to the picture.

Name _____

long

longer

longest

Comparison Adjectives

Write the correct adjective next to the picture.

Name _____

good

better

best

Write the correct comparative adjective in the blank.

Name _____

I had the _____ time ever.

(good)

David is _____ than

(tall)

Susan.

It was the _____

(small)

kitten I had ever seen.

I ate the _____

(big)

ice cream sundae.

Practise by tracing the words.
Then write the words.

Name _____

Dear

Thank you

Sincerely

Your friend

Practise writing a thank-you note.

Name _____

Practise writing a letter.

Name _____

Practise addressing an envelope.

Name _____

Aa

Practise by tracing the letter.
Then write the letter.

Name _____

𝑎 𝑎 𝑎 𝑎 𝑎

𝑎 𝑎 𝑎 𝑎 𝑎

Practise by tracing the words.
Then write the words.

Name _____

an an

and and

animals

April

Write the phrase.

Name _____

Arctic animals

act amusingly

Write the sentence.

Name _____

Arctic animals act amusingly.

Bb

Practise by tracing the letter.
Then write the letter.

Name _____

$\mathcal{B}$ $\mathcal{B}$ $\mathcal{B}$ $\mathcal{B}$ $\mathcal{B}$

$\mathcal{b}$ $\mathcal{b}$ $\mathcal{b}$ $\mathcal{b}$ $\mathcal{b}$

Practise by tracing the words.
Then write the words.

Name _____

big

boy

babble

baboon

Write the phrase.

Name _____

Big baboons

break balloons

Write the sentence.

Name _____

Big baboons

break balloons.

Cc

Practise by tracing the letter.
Then write the letter.

Name _____

$\mathcal{C}$ $\mathcal{C}$ $\mathcal{C}$ $\mathcal{C}$ $\mathcal{C}$ $\mathcal{C}$

$\mathcal{c}$ $\mathcal{c}$ $\mathcal{c}$ $\mathcal{c}$ $\mathcal{c}$

Practise by tracing the words.
Then write the words.

Name _____

can

candy

cool

count

Cc

Write the phrase.

Name _____

Cool crocodiles

count coconuts

Write the sentence.  Name _____

Cool crocodiles count coconuts.

Dd

Practise by tracing the letter.
Then write the letter.

Name _____

Practise by tracing the words.
Then write the words.

Name _____

do

dog

dandelions

donuts

Write the phrase.

Name _____

Dogs deliver

dandelions and

donuts

Write the sentence.

Name _____

Dogs deliver dandelions and donuts.

Ee

Practise by tracing the letter.
Then write the letter.

Name _____

Practise by tracing the words.
Then write the words.

Name _____

each

eat

eels

eighty

Ee

Write the phrase.

Name _____

Electric eels

eat excitedly

Write the sentence.

Name _____

Electric eels eat excitedly.

Ff

Practise by tracing the letter.
Then write the letter.

Name _____

Practise by tracing the words.
Then write the words.

Name _____

far

fat

fluff

feast

Ff

Write the phrase.

Name _____

Flamingos fluff

fancy feathers

Write the sentence.

Name _____

Flamingos fluff fancy feathers.

Gg

Practise by tracing the letter.
Then write the letter.

Name _____

Practise by tracing the words.
Then write the words.

Name _____

gag

gift

good

giggle

Gg

Write the phrase.

Name _____

Giggling gophers

gag gifts

Write the sentence.

Name _____

Giggling gophers give gag gifts.

Hh

Practise by tracing the letter.
Then write the letter.

Name _____

$\mathcal{H}$ $\mathcal{H}$ $\mathcal{H}$ $\mathcal{H}$ $\mathcal{H}$

h h h h h

Practise by tracing the words.
Then write the words.

Name _____

his

happy

he

hello

Hh

Write the phrase.

Name _____

Happy hippos

hang hammocks

Write the sentence.  Name _____

Happy hippos hang in their hammocks.

Practise by tracing the letter.
Then write the letter.

Name _____

Practise by tracing the words.
Then write the words.

Name _____

if

in

idea

itch

Write the phrase.

Name _____

Insects itch

in infield

Write the sentence.  Name _____

Insects itch in the infield.

Jj

Practise by tracing the letter.
Then write the letter.

Name _____

$\mathcal{J}$ $\mathcal{J}$ $\mathcal{J}$ $\mathcal{J}$ $\mathcal{J}$

j j j j j

Practise by tracing the words.
Then write the words.

Name _____

jam

job

jazz

junk

Jj

Write the phrase.

Name _____

Juggling jaguars

to jazz

Write the sentence.

Name _____

Juggling jaguars jam to jazz.

Kk

Practise by tracing the letter.
Then write the letter.

Name _____

$\mathcal{K}$ $\mathcal{K}$ $\mathcal{K}$ $\mathcal{K}$ $\mathcal{K}$

$\mathcal{k}$ $\mathcal{k}$ $\mathcal{k}$ $\mathcal{k}$ $\mathcal{k}$

Practise by tracing the words.
Then write the words.

Name _____

kid

key

kick

keep

Kk

Name _____

Kooky kangaroos

kick karate

Write the sentence.

Name _____

Kooky kangaroos kick in karate.

Practise by tracing the letter.
Then write the letter.

Name _____

$\mathcal{L}$ $\mathcal{L}$ $\mathcal{L}$ $\mathcal{L}$ $\mathcal{L}$ $\mathcal{L}$

ℓ ℓ ℓ ℓ ℓ

Practise by tracing the words.
Then write the words.

Name _____

low

land

lamb

little

LI

Write the phrase.

Name _____

Little lambs

lemon lollipops

Write the sentence.  Name _____

Little lambs lick lemon lollipops.

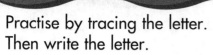

Mm

Practise by tracing the letter.
Then write the letter.

Name _____

m m m m m

m m m m m

Practise by tracing the words.
Then write the words.

Name _____

mad

milk

monkeys

merry

Mm

Write the phrase.

Name _____

Merry monkeys

make marmalade

Write the sentence.  Name _____

Merry monkeys

make marmalade.

ORANGE

Nn

Practise by tracing the letter.
Then write the letter.

Name _____

n n n n n

m m m m m

Practise by tracing the words.
Then write the words.

Name _____

nap

name

near

night

Nn

Write the phrase.

Name _____

naughty gnats

never nap

Write the sentence.  Name _____

Naughty gnats never nap at night.

Practise by tracing the letter.
Then write the letter.

Name _____

Practise by tracing the words.
Then write the words.

Name _____

out

often

once

order

Oo

Write the phrase.

Name _____

Ostriches often

onion omelettes

Write the sentence.

Name _____

Oo

Ostriches often order onion omelettes.

MENU

egg omelette

Pp

Practise by tracing the letter.
Then write the letter.

Name _____

𝓟 𝓟 𝓟 𝓟 𝓟

𝓅 𝓅 𝓅 𝓅 𝓅

Practise by tracing the words.
Then write the words.

Name _____

pan

pet

pick

paper

Pp

Name _____

Pandas paint

pictures paper

Write the sentence.  Name _____

Pandas paint pictures on paper.

Qq

Practise by tracing the letter.
Then write the letter.

Name _____

Q Q Q Q Q

q q q q q

Practise by tracing the words.
Then write the words.

Name _____

quit

quick

queen

quiet

Qq

Write the phrase.  Name _____

Quick quails

unique quarter

Write the sentence.

Name _____

Quick quails quarrel over a unique quarter.

Rr

Practise by tracing the letter.
Then write the letter.

Name _____

Rr

Practise by tracing the words.
Then write the words.

Name _____

rat

run

rear

road

Rr

Name _____

Raccoons run

red cars

Write the sentence.

Name _____

Raccoons run races in red cars.

Ss

Practise by tracing the letter.
Then write the letter.

Name _____

Practise by tracing the words.
Then write the words.

Name _____

see

sing

stand

stow

Ss

Write the phrase.

Name _____

Standing storks

sing swans

Write the sentence.

Name _____

Standing storks

sing with swans.

Practise by tracing the letter.
Then write the letter.

Name _____

$\mathcal{T}$ $\mathcal{T}$ $\mathcal{T}$ $\mathcal{T}$ $\mathcal{T}$

$\mathcal{t}$ $\mathcal{t}$ $\mathcal{t}$ $\mathcal{t}$ $\mathcal{t}$

Tt

Practise by tracing the words.
Then write the words.

Name _____

the

tip

told

twist

259

Write the phrase.

Name _____

Two tigers

tickle toes

Tt

Write the sentence.

Name _____

Two tigers tickle each other's toes.

Uu

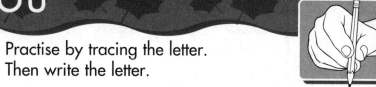

Practise by tracing the letter.
Then write the letter.

Name _____

$\mathcal{U}$ $\mathcal{U}$ $\mathcal{U}$ $\mathcal{U}$ $\mathcal{U}$

$\mathcal{u}$ $\mathcal{u}$ $\mathcal{u}$ $\mathcal{u}$ $\mathcal{u}$

Practise by tracing the words.
Then write the words.

Name _____

use

under

until

unhappy

Uu

Write the phrase.

Name _____

Unicorns use

umbrellas under

Write the sentence.

Name _____

Unicorns use umbrellas under thunder.

265

Vv

Practise by tracing the letter.
Then write the letter.

Name _____

$\mathcal{V}$ $\mathcal{V}$ $\mathcal{V}$ $\mathcal{V}$ $\mathcal{V}$

v v v v v

Practise by tracing the words.
Then write the words.

Name _____

very

vote

vine

vest

Vv

Write the phrase.

Name _____

Vultures vacuum

velvet vests

Write the sentence.

Name _____

Vultures vacuum in velvet vests.

Ww

Practise by tracing the letter.
Then write the letter.

Name _____

$\mathcal{W}$ $\mathcal{W}$ $\mathcal{W}$ $\mathcal{W}$ $\mathcal{W}$

w w w w w

Practise by tracing the words.
Then write the words.

Name _____

wet

west

wall

winter

Ww

Write the phrase.

Name _____

Wet walruses

to win

Write the sentence.

Name _____

Wet walruses bowl to win.

Xx

Practise by tracing the letter.
Then write the letter.

Name _____

X X X X X

x x x x x

274

Practise by tracing the words.
Then write the words.

Name _____

x-ray

box

extra

xylophone

X-RAY
MACHINE

FOX IN BOX

Write the phrase.

Name _____

x-ray boxes

with foxes

Write the sentence.  Name _____

Xandra x-rays boxes with foxes.

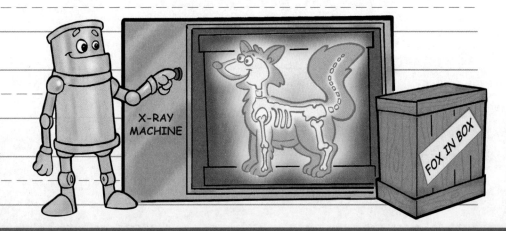

X-RAY MACHINE

FOX IN BOX

Yy

Practise by tracing the letter.
Then write the letter.

Name _____

$\mathcal{Y}$ $\mathcal{Y}$ $\mathcal{Y}$ $\mathcal{Y}$ $\mathcal{Y}$ $\mathcal{Y}$

$\mathcal{y}$ $\mathcal{y}$ $\mathcal{y}$ $\mathcal{y}$ $\mathcal{y}$

Practise by tracing the words.
Then write the words.

Name _____

you

yard

year

yellow

Yy

Name _____

Yaks yell

Yodel loudly

Write the sentence.  Name _____

Yaks yell and yodel loudly.

Zz

Practise by tracing the letter.
Then write the letter.

Name _____

Practise by tracing the words.
Then write the words.

Name _____

zero

zoom

zone

zipper

Zz

Write the phrase.

Name _____

zigzagging zebras

zip zoom

Zz

Write the sentence.

Name _____

Zigzagging zebras zip and zoom.

285

Practise by tracing the words and numbers. Then write the words and numbers.

Name _____

one 1

two 2

three 3

four 4

five 5

Practise by tracing the words and numbers. Then write the words and numbers.

Name _____

six 6

seven 7

eight 8

nine 9

ten 10

Practise by tracing the words and numbers. Then write the words and numbers.

Name _____

eleven 11

twelve 12

thirteen 13

fourteen 14

fifteen 15

Practise by tracing the words and numbers. Then write the words and numbers.

Name _____

sixteen 16

seventeen 17

eighteen 18

nineteen 19

twenty 20

Shape Words

Practise by tracing the words.
Then write the words.

Name _____

square

circle

rectangle

oval

Practise by tracing the words.
Then write the words.

Name _____

red

blue

yellow

orange

Practise by tracing the words.
Then write the words.

Name _____

black

white

purple

pink

Practise by tracing the words.
Then write the words.

Name _____

brown

grey

green

Complete this sentence:

My favourite

colour is _____.

Name _____

Practise by tracing the words and abbreviations. Then write the words and abbreviations.

Sunday

Sun.

Monday

Mon.

Practise by tracing the words and abbreviations. Then write the words and abbreviations.

Name _____

Tuesday

Tues.

Wednesday

Wed.

Practise by tracing the words and abbreviations. Then write the words and abbreviations.

Name _____

Thursday

Thurs.

Friday

Fri.

Practise by tracing the words and abbreviations. Then write the words and abbreviations.

Name _____

Saturday

Sat.

Today

Practise by tracing the words and abbreviations. Then write the words and abbreviations.

Name _____

January

Jan.

February

Feb.

Practise by tracing the words and abbreviations. Then write the words and abbreviations.

Name _____

March

Mar.

April

Apr.

Months of the Year
and Abbreviations

Practise by tracing the words and abbreviations. Then write the words and abbreviations.

Name _____

May

June

July

August

Aug.

Practise by tracing the words and abbreviations. Then write the words and abbreviations.

Name _____

September

Sept.

October

Oct.

Practise by tracing the words and abbreviations. Then write the words and abbreviations.

Name _____

November

Nov.

December

Dec.

Practise by tracing the words.
Then write the words.

Name _____

winter

spring

summer

fall

Weather Words

Practise by tracing the words.
Then write the words.

snow

rain

sunshine

sleet

Complete this sentence:

Today we have

Practise by tracing the words.
Then write the words.

Name _____

Halloween

Easter

Canada Day

Hanukkah

Practise by tracing the words.
Then write the words.

Name _____

Christmas

Valetine's Day

Kwanza

Happy Birthday

Practise by tracing the words.
Then write the words.

Name _____

gym

playground

classroom

principal's office

Practise by tracing the words.
Then write the words.

Name _____

math

music

art

reading

Practise by tracing the words.
Then write the words.

Name _____

science

spelling

social studies

writing

Practise by tracing the words.
Then write the words.

Name _____

teacher

aide

nurse

principal

Practise by tracing the words.
Then write the words.

Name _____

pencil

book

folder

paper

Practise by tracing the words.
Then write the words.

Name _____

stop

go

caution

Practise by tracing the words.
Then write the words.

Name _____

Mother

Father

Mom

Practise by tracing the words.
Then write the words.

Name _____

Dad

Grandma

Grandpa

Practise by tracing the words.
Then write the words.

Name _____

aunt

uncle

brother

sister

Write the names of the people in your family.

Name _____

Practise by tracing the words.
Then write the words.

Name _____

street

road

store

theatre

Practise by tracing the words.
Then write the words.

Name _____

apartment

library

office

park

Complete these sentences:

Name _____

I live in a

_____.

My address is

_____.

Write a sentence about your neighbourhood:

Practise by tracing the words.
Then write the words.

Name _____

dollar $

cents ¢

penny 1¢

Practise by tracing the words.
Then write the words.

Name _____

nickel 5¢

dime 10¢

quarter 25¢

Practise by tracing the words.
Then write the words.

Name _____

_____

_ _ _ _ _ _ _ _ _ _ _ _ _ _ _ _ _ _

_____

_____

_ _ _ _ _ _ _ _ _ _ _ _ _ _ _ _ _ _

_____

_____

_ _ _ _ _ _ _ _ _ _ _ _ _ _ _ _ _ _

_____

_____

_ _ _ _ _ _ _ _ _ _ _ _ _ _ _ _ _ _

_____

_____

_ _ _ _ _ _ _ _ _ _ _ _ _ _ _ _ _ _

_____

_____

_ _ _ _ _ _ _ _ _ _ _ _ _ _ _ _ _ _

_____

_____

_ _ _ _ _ _ _ _ _ _ _ _ _ _ _ _ _ _

_____

_____

_ _ _ _ _ _ _ _ _ _ _ _ _ _ _ _ _ _

_____

_____

_ _ _ _ _ _ _ _ _ _ _ _ _ _ _ _ _ _

_____

_____

_ _ _ _ _ _ _ _ _ _ _ _ _ _ _ _ _ _

_____

Practise by tracing the words.
Then write the words.

Name _____

run

swim

jump

fly

Practise by tracing the words.
Then write the words.

Name _____

sing

read

play

study

Practise by tracing the words.
Then write the words.

Name _____

big

long

tall

good

Write the correct adjective
next to the picture.

Name _____

tall

taller

tallest

Write the correct adjective
next to the picture.

Name _____

big

bigger

biggest

_____

Comparison Adjectives

Write the correct adjective next to the picture.

Name _____

small

smaller

smallest

Write the correct adjective
next to the picture.

Name _____

long

longer

longest

Comparison Adjectives

Write the correct adjective next to the picture.

Name _____

good

better

best

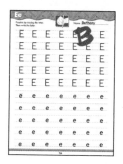

Write the correct comparative
adjective in the blank.

Name _____

I had the _____
(good)

time ever.

David is _____
(tall)

than Susan.

It was the

_____ *kitten*
(small)

I had ever seen.

I ate the _____
(big)

ice cream sundae.

Practise by tracing the words.
Then write the words.

Name _____

Dear

Thank you

Sincerely

Your friend

Practise writing a thank-you note.

Name _____

Practise writing a letter
to your friend.

Name _____

Practise by tracing the words.
Then write the words.

Name _____

dictionary

definition

alphabetical order

Pronouns

Practise by tracing the words.
Then write the words.

Name _____

I

me

you

her

we

Practise by tracing the words.
Then write the words.

Name _____

he

she

they

them

Practise by tracing the words.
Then write the words.

Name _____

I'll

she'll

we'll

you'll

Practise by tracing the words.
Then write the words.

Name _____

sentence

paragraph

poem

story

Complete these sentences:

Name _____

At the end of a
_____. you
put a period.

A _____
has a main idea.

A _____ does not
have to rhyme.

A _____ has a
beginning, middle,
and end.

Practise by tracing the words.
Then write the words.

Name _____

fiction

nonfiction

biography

autobiography

Complete these sentences:

Name _____

A _____ book
tells about things
that really
happened.

A _____ book
tells a story
that is not real.

A _____
tells the story of
someone's life.

Practise by tracing the words.
Then write the words.

Name _____

add

subtract

multiply

divide

Practise by tracing the words.
Then write the words.

Name _____

sum

product

regrouping

Complete this sentence:

When you add,

the answer is

called a _____.

Practise by tracing the words.
Then write the words.

Name _____

one-half

one-fourth

one-eighth

three-quarters

Use words from the previous page to complete these sentences:

Name _____

There is _____

glass of milk left.

The pizza is

_____

gone.

There is only

_____ *of the*

pizza left.

Practise by tracing the words.
Then write the words.

Name _____

millimetre

centimetre

metre

decimetre

kilometre

Complete these sentences:

Name _____

There are ten millimetres in a _____.

There are one hundred _____ in a _____.

There are one thousand metres in a _____.

Practise by tracing the words.
Then write the words.

Name _____

habitat

experiment

food chain

water cycle

Practise by tracing the words.
Then write the words.

Name _____

paint

draw

sketch

sculpture

**Practise by tracing the words.
Then write the words.**

Name _____

sing

piano

note

strings

Practise by tracing the words.
Then write the words.

Name _____

band

violin

drums

trumpet